Table of Contents

Clutter Control: How to Get Rid of Clutter, Organize Your Home, Workplace and Life, Focus on Important Things

By Angela Pierce

Introduction

Sometimes the constant hustle and bustle of everyday life gets the best of us. While we are busy focusing on our careers and juggling the long hours and multiple responsibilities with our hectic family and home lives, things can get tossed aside and forgotten about. Bills and other opened and unopened mail can pile up on your counter or be shoved in drawers. Your bookshelves and magazine racks are overflowing and in disarray. Your child's toys are piled up in the living room and dirty clothes can turn your stairs into an obstacle course. When you are able to catch your breath, you realize that you have a clutter problem.

While clutter can be a common occurrence in a household, allowing clutter to continue and get worse can cause many problems. Clutter can cause great stress and can unduly affect your overall mood. Not only does clutter drain your energy and cause frustration, it can make it more difficult to get things done. Ultimately, clutter can overwhelm you and your family and it significantly impacts the overall physical and mental health of your family. To gain control over clutter and to take back control, you need to understand what clutter is and what is symbolizes. Furthermore, you need to have the tools and vision to help make clutter a thing of the past.

Chapter 1. Clutter Basics

While many people may define clutter as simply a mess, there is a deeper significance to what is defined as clutter. First, clutter can be defined as a place or state that is jumbled, confused and disorderly. Clutter can also be defined as something that is made disorderly by covering or filling up with objects. Clutter doesn't just refer to our households; it can also extend into our daily plans, your work space and your overall mindset. While clutter is detrimental in the fact there is a physical sense of chaos and disorder, there is mental side to clutter that needs to be acknowledged. While we focus on the clutter we have in our homes and workplace, it can diminish our capacity to accomplish things, diminishes our passions and desires and hinders how we can adequately help and serve others.

Are There Different Types of Clutter?

It may be difficult to know what qualifies as clutter, because clutter can be seen as subjective and dependent on the eye of the beholder. What one person defines as clutter another person may define as treasure. In general, clutter can be categorized into two general categories: memory clutter and what is referred to as 'someday' clutter.

Memory clutter can be defined as those items that remind us of important life events and have significant emotional attachment. Examples of memory clutter can include keepsakes or heirlooms, old photographs, children's toys and clothes, and even old college textbooks. People are hesitant to remove memory clutter because they fear they will lose the memories attached to these items.

Someday clutter refers to those items that you are reluctant to throw away because you may have a use for them down the road. An example of someday clutter can be clothes in the closet that haven't been thrown out because you may think you will fit into them again. Another example of this form of clutter is an old project from a hobby long forgotten that you have been meaning to complete. With someday clutter, the "maybe" we are thinking about get put off and forgotten about and turns into a "never".

Clutter Control:

How to Get Rid of Clutter, Organize Your Home, Workplace and Life, Focus on Important Things

By

Angela Pierce

Chapter 2. Dangers of Clutter

Reasons Why Clutter Causes Stress

When we have spaces that are cluttered, it impacts how we feel about our homes, where we work, how our family feels and ultimately how we feel. While the mess in our homes and workplaces make us feel overwhelmed and anxious, clutter is not widely recognized as a major contributor to stress. The main way clutter impacts our lives is how it bombards our minds with its presence. The sights, sounds and smells of clutter overwhelm our senses with stimuli. Because we focus so much of our attention of the clutter, we lose focus on other important aspects of our lives.

Because clutter can be overwhelming, aren't able to either physically or mentally relax and the presence of clutter tells our mind that our work will never be done. Clutter can also make us anxious and hesitant in organizing because of the fear of what we might find at the bottom of the pile. Additionally, clutter produces feelings of extreme guilt because we feel that we should be more organized and are embarrassed when family and other house guest come visit. Since clutter takes up significant portions of open spaces in our homes and offices, our abilities to problem solve and think are stifled because we need those open spaces to roam and pace.

Can Clutter Be Dangerous?

If we fail to organize what is cluttered and employ a carefully thought out plan to manage our households, the clutter that has accumulated has the potential to be dangerous to both the health and overall safety of you and your family. In case of a fire or other emergency, excess clutter can provide obstacles to exits and family members can trip over piles and become injured and can actually make these emergency situations worse. If medical personnel have to come to your home, they may have difficulty in using a stretcher or other essential medical equipment. When clutter is present, the overall health quality of your home or workspace diminishes and there can be the potential for health complications to arise.

Chapter 3. Simple Ways to Get Rid of Clutter in Your Home

Oftentimes the best ways to get rid of clutter and to organize your home is by finding a few minutes in your day. The process of removing clutter from your home can be stressful and overwhelming, but there are some simple steps that you can take on a daily basis that only take a few minutes and can save you the stress and headaches that can happen if you let things slide too far. Instead of focusing on your entire home or apartment, find one or two of your most problem areas and work to clean and organize those areas.

If you have five minutes a day to spare, you can focus on throwing out any old or crusty kitchen sponges and you can go through your refrigerator and toss out old leftovers and check for food products that are outdated. In that five minutes you can also go through your medicine cabinet and throw away any cosmetics or over-the-counter medicines that may be expired. If you are in your living room, you can use five minutes or the times between commercial breaks to gather magazines, throw miscellaneous garbage in the trash and give the living room a quick vacuum.

If you have a little more time in your day, an easy clutter removal and organizing activity is to select a cabinet or closet that is troublesome. Take everything out of that space and arrange them into three separate piles. One pile should contains items that you always use, another pile should contain items that see occasional or seasonal use and the third pile should have rarely or never used items. When you sort these items, the rarely or never used items can be tossed or given away unless they have sentimental value or have considerable monetary worth. Seasonal items should be placed in the back of the storage area while your commonly used items are placed towards the front so you can use them right away.

Chapter 4. Step-by-Step Tips on Removing Clutter and Organizing Your Entire Living Space

When clutter takes over a specific living space, it is often have a snowball effect for the rest of your house or apartment. As stated several times in this book, widespread clutter can be overwhelming. Trying to sort, purge and reorganize your entire living space in one fell swoop is an impossible feat and oftentimes people abandon this project which allows the problem to become worse. In order to effectively remove clutter and reorganize your home or apartment, it takes detailed planning and careful thought. The following are some tips that will help you better organize this undertaking and help alleviate stress and worry.

Change Your Mindset and Habits

For you to effectively deal with clutter and have a more organized living space, you need to think differently about clutter. As alluded to earlier, getting into the habit of throwing out junk items and organizing on the spot can establish new and healthier cleaning habits. A simple habit that people can pick up is to pick up the first thing they see and either putting it where it belongs or finding a new home for that particular item. When confronted with a larger cleaning and organizing project, it is important to think small.

Pick an area or a room and think about what your room should look like and try to leave any emotional attachments to particular items out of the thought process. Starting small makes the job of clutter control easier on your mind and in your soul. If possible, get your family involved in the process. Assigning responsibility and following up reinforces the fact that cleaning and organizing the household is the responsibility of all members of the family.

Pick a Space and Get to Work

Once you have changed your mindset to your clutter and have gone around and evaluated your living space, pick an area of your house or apartment are start working. A common area that experiences a lot of clutter are desktops. You need to carefully go through the items on your desktop, since there may be bills and other important documents that you can't throw away.

If you have a copy of a bill that has been already paid throw it away immediately, and the same holds true for other non-essential paperwork. For those important documents that cannot be thrown away, it is extremely important to separate those items and put them somewhere safe where there is no danger for them being thrown away. Marking them by a bright Post-it or putting in a colored folder that is clearly marked are good suggestions.

If you still have clutter issues after this initial purge and organization, you can look at integrating organizational, space saving solutions that will better organize your belongings while making your space look visually appealing. Some common options include small desks, filing cabinets, shelving or decorative totes. If you utilize these space saving items, it is important to clearly mark what is contained in each item. For example, you should alphabetize documents and forms if you use a filing cabinet, or clearly mark what each section contains for easy reference. You can employ this process in a similar fashion for the other rooms of your living space.

Be Able to Identify the Where Your Clutter Comes From

As you work through your clutter it is important to determine where items in those piles are come from in your home or apartment. Along with bills and other paperwork, these clutter piles can also contain laundry, children's artwork, tools and other hardware, electronic devices and are miscellaneous household items. Being able to identify the sources where your clutter comes from will allow you to place them back to where they belong, or you can create new storage solutions to store those items.

Get Rid of That "Someday" Clutter

If you have excess clothes that are overwhelming your closet or have appliances that you seldom or never use it is best to simply get rid of those items. A good rule of thumb is to throw away those items that you haven't used or thought about for at least a year. You can sell those items to make some extra money or you can simply give the items away to friends or family. No matter what method you decide to use, be sure you get rid of the item or items.

How to Deal With Memory Clutter

If you are going through items that have great sentimental value, the process of throwing them can be highly emotional. Getting rid of items that mean a lot to you and evoke a lot of emotion is difficult, but you need to try and simplify and keep in mind that the history behind those items is more important than the item itself. You can try and pare down these items and display those with have the most sentimental value to you. The items that mean the most might be found in a random box in a closet or attic space. Sort through those boxes and keep only those items that have the strongest emotional attachment. You can also give items to family members or friends to keep safe.

You can also give away some of your more ordinary items in order to keep those with high sentimental value. Examples include fine china that belonged to your grandmother or a pearl necklace that was given to you as a wedding gift. Try to find uses for those sentimental items on a more regular basis. You can also look to sort through old photographs and digitize them. You can also take pictures of those prized possessions and create a digital photo book and then discard those items if you wish.

Make Space for Your Essentials

Oftentimes everyday items such as keys, wallets and cell phones can add to our clutter and we experience great anxiety if we are unable to find these items. For peace of mind, find a common place to store these items and make it a habit to place those items in those places every time you come home. You can use a front entry table, an available cubby hole or create shelf space.

Replace Old with New (and Make it Functional)

If you buy an item such an appliance or item of clothing, be sure you get rid of similar items that are older. The process of cycling through items is an excellent ongoing maintenance procedure that can reduce clutter in your home. You also want to buy items that can perform multiple functions. For example, if you buy a blender that can act as a juicer or a food processor you don't need to have these separate items. This creates more space and organization.

Create Storage Spaces

In order to help contain clutter, we can incorporate simple, built-in design features or use what is readily available to create secondary features that can be used to store items. For example, it is estimated that half the items that we take with us never stay by the front door when we return. For items such as coats, hats, purses and shopping bags, creating a mudroom can help reduce the amount of clutter that is relegated to a front closet. Mudrooms are usually small rooms or entryways where items such as footwear and outerwear are placed. Additionally, you can incorporate built-in storage spaces that feature multiple compartments and doors. These features can built right into your wall can provide you with the necessary storage space that you need while giving your living spaces a clean and presentable look.

Don't Buy Things You Will Use One Time

A common clutter culprit are items that may have been used only one time and then forgotten about over time. A prime example of these items include power tools and other household tools. These tools can often be borrowed or rented if they are only needed on a temporary basis.

Consider Quality over Quantity

During holidays and other times were gift giving is normal, it is important to keep in mind that it isn't the number of gifts that are given and received but the thought behind those gifts. To cut down on the number of gifts that can be unused and turn to clutter, have family members provide you a list of items they really need. Additionally, you can utilize a registry for gift giving or you can ask family members to chip in to get one big gift.

If Possible, Get Rid of Old Music and Movies

In today's advanced technological age, there are many companies which provide online movie streaming services. Additionally, with devices such as iPads and iPods, it is possible to store thousands of song titles and albums. You can utilize these services and sell, donate your movies, CD's and playing devices.

Organize Your Garage

Whether you think about it or not, your garage is technically a room of your house. You can utilize the same storage options and solutions that you use in your home to organize your garage. By organizing your garage, you not only take care of clutter issues in that space, but you can also help alleviate any clutter issues that are found throughout your home.

Go Vertical if You Have a Small Living Space

If you live in a home or apartment with limited square footage, the storage space that you need will have to go up and not out. With vertical storage options such as shelves, it takes up less floor space will help make your overall living space less cluttered.

Purge, Sell, Donate

In order to help maintain order and organization, you should organize seasonal cleaning during the spring and fall. You can take excess items and donate them to charity, take them to a consignment store or hold a semi-annual yard sale. Additionally, having a donation box in your garage can be a place where family members can drop off items they no longer use. When the box is full, it can be taken to the Salvation Army, donated to charity or given away to friends and co-workers who may need those items.

Buy Multipurpose Furniture

If possible, buy pieces of furniture that can be used in multiple ways. For example, you can buy a trunk or chest that can also be used as a coffee table or have a bench that can compartments for storage. Having items that serve multiple purposes can preserve valuable floor space and reduce clutter.

Chapter 5. Removing Clutter and Improving Organization at Your Workplace

Removing clutter and embracing organization is not just for your home; it can also benefit you at your workplace. Since you are relegated to the relatively small space of your office or desk, having a neat an organized spot is essential for your peace of mind and productivity. The following are some basic tips that will help reduce clutter at your office or work space.

Find a Place for Every Item

While the process of finding a place for everything, remembering to put those items back can be a challenge with all that goes on at work on a daily basis. Start small with your pens and pencils by placing them in an unused coffee cup or holder. Once you have a place for your pens, you can put related items such as Post-It notes near the pens so you have easy access to them when you need to jot something down.

While they are convenient, Post-It notes can cause clutter if not thrown away at the end of the day. If you use a Post-It note for quickly writing down a short daily to-do list or to mark a page in your planner or a book, be sure to throw them away at the end of the day. In regards to other common items such as calendars, you want to move them to a shelf, pin them to a corkboard display on a wall near you, or get a desktop calendar.

Establish an Inbox/Outbox System

If your job requires you to work with a lot of paper documents, having an inbox/outbox type of organizational system can help prioritize your work and reduce clutter. The inbox can be designated for projects and tasks that you are currently working while outboxes can be designated for items that have been completed, need to be filed or passed on to another department. This type of system can be utilized by the use of stackable trays that are clearly marked.

Display Your Best Items

While it is important to decorate your desk with items that will make you feel comfortable, too many items can overwhelm you and distract you from doing your job. Keep it simple with a nice framed photo of your dog or children, plant or other memento. If there is any miscellaneous clutter such as paper clips and erasers have a dedicated portion of your desk for those items. If needed, mark down those spaces in your desk where certain items need to go.

Use a Notebook

You need to have a method for organizing your thoughts and laying out the important tasks of your work day. Having a spiral notebook is a great tool to right down these important thoughts and tasks. In the notebook, you can make space for your primary and secondary to do lists and edit them as you go. This could save on your use of Post-It notes and thereby reduce your clutter. Additionally, you are able to multi-task better and more efficiently and if you get interrupted or have a random thought about a different project or task, you can jot it down for later use.

Tips Regarding the Regular Cleaning of Your Office Space

Much like the seasonal purging and cleaning at your home or apartment, you need to do the same at your office. You should clean and organize your office once a month if possible and when you do so your must carefully plan this event. You should find a slow time of the day or do this regular cleaning before or after office hours. When you choose a day to perform a more comprehensive cleaning and organizing of your office you should block out two hours to complete this task.

Before you begin cleaning and organizing, you will need to have supplies such as the following:

*Windex or similar cleaners and paper towels

*Colored folders

*Three cardboard boxes

*Pencils and markers

*File boxes, drawers or vertical stackers

You will need to determine which area of your office space or desk you will clean first. Once that is determined, you will first take items off of your desk and place them into one cardboard box. You will next empty your drawers into another box. You will sort the contents of the two boxes and take your papers or documents and place them into colored folders that denote what is contained in them and placing them back into the filing cabinet. You should write in pencil what each folder is until you are able to finalize what should be in each colored folder. You will also throw or discard any old or unused desk items.

If there are paper items that have duplicates online or on a folder in the desktop of your computer, you do not need to keep paper copies of those items. Anything that is left over can be placed in placed in the third box and be dealt with later. Do not empty all of your drawers at once! Start with a couple of drawers and work through those. If you get interrupted, you will have less of a mess on your hands. Additionally, you should institute a daily and weekly cleaning and maintenance schedule to keep your office space free of clutter.

Chapter 6. Clutter Control Is The Key to Organization, Efficiency and Peace of Mind

The ability to efficiently deal with clutter and organizing your living and work spaces will not only make those spaces visually appealing, you will be able to find things quickly and be able to perform tasks in a more efficient manner. With a clean and organized space that is free of clutter, it will also reduce your stress and provide you with a safer environment for you and your family in your home or apartment, and provide a more efficient work environment. By utilizing the tips and suggestions listed above, you will be well on your way to a better looking and functioning environment for your home, apartment and office.

I want to personally thank you for reading my book. I hope you found information in this book useful and I would be very grateful if you could leave your honest review about this book. I certainly want to thank you in advance for doing this.